World Faiths Today Series
Exploring the Orthodox Church

Who are your friends? Do you know everything about them? Do they know everything about you?

Well, this is a story about friends who know everything about one another. But they are still learning about what their friends do and why they do them. Read their story and you might learn something new too!

1 Visiting the Orthodox church

Rees and Sara enjoyed visiting their local corner shop. The shop sold almost everything, with the shelves, the floor, and the counter all stocked with interesting things. It was run by Mr and Mrs Maslov. Their children, Anna and Michael, went to school with Rees and Sara, and they were friends.

Both Anna and Michael's grandparents had grown up in Russia, and the whole family had remained members of the Eastern Orthodox Church. Now that they are living in Wales they have to drive many miles to attend the nearest Eastern Orthodox church. It is very important for them to make this journey as often as they can.

On Sunday the corner shop is often run by other people so that Mr and Mrs Maslov, Anna, and Michael can go off to their church. It takes them about an hour and a half each way.

Anna and Michael had told Rees and Sara all about their church, but Rees and Sara had never been there. All of this was going to change, because Mr and Mrs Maslov had planned to take Rees and Sara with them the following Sunday.

The following Sunday when Mr and Mrs Maslov's car drew up outside the church, Rees and Sara felt disappointed. They had expected the Eastern Orthodox church to look quite different from anything they had ever seen before. Instead it looked just like any other church.

Anna spotted her friends' look of disappointment. 'This church was first built by the Anglicans over a hundred years ago. The Eastern Orthodox congregation bought it quite recently. Outside it looks like any other church, but wait until you go inside!' she said.

Rees and Sara followed their friends to the church door, not knowing at all what to expect.

Anna and Michael held the door open and let their friends walk in first. As soon as Rees and Sara stepped inside their faces lit up with excitement.

The church smelled very different from anything they had ever smelled before. The air was heavy with the rich smell of incense.

The church sounded very different from anything they had ever heard before. The choir was already singing the most beautiful Eastern Orthodox chant.

The church looked very different from anything they had ever seen before. Their eyes were immediately caught by the solid wooden screen at the front and the beautiful pictures hanging there.

Michael nudged Rees. 'Pay attention,' he laughed, 'and watch what we do.'

'First of all,' said Michael, 'we make the sign of the cross.' He held the thumb and first two fingers of his right hand bunched together, and held the other two fingers close to his palm. He brought his thumb and first two fingers to his forehead, then to his chest, to his right shoulder, and last of all to his left shoulder. He looked very serious.

'Next,' said Michael, 'we light a candle. You can light one, too. Follow us!' Rees and Sara did what their friends did. They lit a candle and carried it slowly to the front of the church. There they placed their candle before the screen.

Looking up, Rees and Sara gazed at the beautiful pictures.

'Now,' said Michael, 'we kiss the pictures. We call them icons. They show the saints in heaven.' Rees and Sara felt very special as they kissed the beautiful pictures.

The solid wooden icon screen divided the church into two parts.

'We stay this side of the screen with the rest of the congregation,' said Michael. 'This symbolises that we are on earth. On the other side of the screen is the altar and that symbolises heaven. Only the priest can go there. The priest moves between heaven and earth, working to bring God and people closer together.'

Rees and Sara gazed with curiosity at the richly painted ceiling and at the richly painted wall behind the altar.

'It feels like a gateway to heaven,' murmured Rees.

The visit to the Eastern Orthodox church had taught Rees and Sara something new about their friends. Anna and Michael believe that their church brings people closer to God, with the help of the saints and the priest celebrating the sacraments. This is so important to them that the family makes a big effort to attend church services.

2 Celebrating Easter

Anna and Michael had invited Rees and Sara to go back to their church. This time the service was not at 10.30 on a Sunday morning, but at 11.30 on a Saturday night. They were on their way to the Easter service, although Rees and Sara had had their Easter eggs several Sundays earlier.

'The Eastern Orthodox Church keeps Easter at a different time from the other churches around here,' explained Anna.

As they drove through the night, Anna and Michael told Rees and Sara about the Easter story. 'The gospels tell us that Jesus was put to death on Good Friday,' said Anna. 'He was crucified on the cross. Afterwards his friends took his body, and placed it in a tomb. A big stone was placed over the entrance to the tomb.'

'Jesus was in the tomb all Saturday,' added Michael.

'But over Saturday night something very strange happened,' continued Anna. 'The stone was rolled away. Jesus' friends came, while it was still dark, but the body had gone. Tonight we are going to see what happened.'

When Mr and Mrs Maslov's car stopped outside, the church was in darkness. 'Do not go in yet,' whispered Anna to Rees and Sara. 'Let's go over there and wait.'

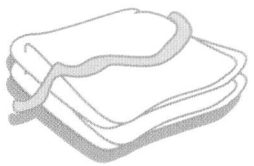

As midnight approached, a long procession of people, with the priest in front, came out from the church.

Everyone standing outside in the cool night air took a lighted candle to join the procession. Rees and Sara did so as well.

At the stroke of midnight the priest chanted the Easter hymn three times.

> Christ is risen from the dead:
> Trampling down death by death:
> And on those in the tombs bestowing life.

The people repeated the hymn. Bells were rung. The joyous news of Easter was proclaimed. The doors of the church were opened again and the priest and the people processed into the building. The church was now flooded with light.

Inside the people greeted each other by saying, 'Christ is risen!' Others replied, 'He is risen indeed!'

During the service, Rees and Sara looked carefully at the solid wooden icon screen in front of them. There were three openings in the screen. The two openings at either end held large doors. The priest opened these doors to pass to and fro between the altar and the people, making his journey between heaven and earth. He always closed the doors behind him.

The centre opening was very special. The top half was closed off by curtains. By opening the curtains the priest allowed the people to glimpse what was going on behind the screen. The bottom half was closed by double wooden doors. By opening these doors the priest allowed the people to see even more.

Whenever the priest pulled back the curtains and opened the doors, Rees and Sara craned their necks to see what was happening.

When the service was over, Rees and Sara joined their friends for the Easter breakfast. It was now 3.00 in the morning. They were given Easter eggs, but these were no ordinary Easter eggs. They were not made from chocolate. They were real hard-boiled eggs that had been dyed in bright colours. Anna and Michael knocked their eggs together hard to try to crack them. 'Christ is risen!' said Anna.

'He is risen indeed!' responded Michael.

Then Michael knocked Sara's bright blue egg. 'Christ is risen!' said Michael.

'He is risen indeed!' replied Sara.

Rees knocked Anna's bright red egg. 'Christ is risen!' said Rees.

'He is risen indeed!' responded Anna.

Around that special Easter breakfast table the brightly coloured eggs proclaimed to everyone the good news of new life, the good news of Christ's victory over death.

Around that special Easter breakfast table there were other special foods as well. 'During the forty days before Easter, we have kept a fast and not eaten rich foods,' said Anna. 'Now on Easter morning our fast has ended so we eat to celebrate.'

When Rees and Sara got home on Sunday morning, they were very tired. But they were happy because they had learnt so much about Anna and Michael's Easter celebrations. In the Eastern Orthodox Church Easter is a very special festival. It celebrates and proclaims the good news that Jesus has risen from the dead. Anna and Michael believe that through Jesus' death on the cross and his resurrection, he offers eternal life to all who follow him.

3 Studying the icons

Rees and Sara were really fascinated by the solid wooden icon screen in the church. Their friends Anna and Michael had explained to them how each icon presents one of the holy saints of the church who live close to God.

When Rees and Sara went to visit Anna and Michael's home, they found icons there as well. There were icons in the hall, in the kitchen, and even in the bedrooms.

Seeing the icon in Anna's bedroom, Sara said, 'That picture is really lovely. Tell us about your icons.'

'That icon is Saint Anna, after whom I was given my name,' said Anna. 'It is very beautiful, but we do not use icons like pictures for decorations. Icons help us to see the holiness of the saints. Icons help us to pray. Icons draw us closer to God. The haloes of light which are painted around their heads are symbols of God's presence with the saints.'

Rees and Sara looked carefully and saw the bright halo around Saint Anna's head.

'When we stand before the icon,' said Anna, 'we can feel Saint Anna is really here with us.'

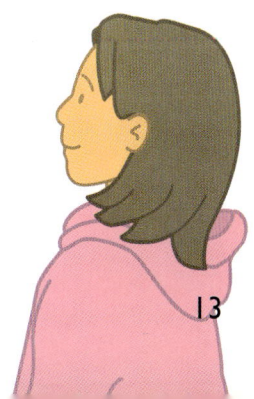

Michael took up the story where Anna had left off. 'I remember seeing an icon being painted,' said Michael. 'Before starting, the iconographer prayed to God. Then he carried out his work with great care and devotion. When he had finished, the iconographer did not write his name on his work. He had painted the icon for the glory of God, not for his own glory.'

Rees and Sara thought the iconographer must have been a very special sort of person. After a short pause, Anna chipped in, 'The priest taught us that icons have to be blessed with holy water before they are ready to hang in our churches or in our homes.'

Then Anna and Michael led the way downstairs and into the kitchen.

In the kitchen, Anna and Michael pointed to an icon of a holy-looking man, with a halo of light around his head. 'Here is one of the ancient saints of Wales,' said Michael. 'Here is Saint Cadwaladr, the last Celtic King of Britain.'

'Cadwaladr never really wanted to be king,' added Anna. 'He was not a warrior like his father. He was a meek and humble man.'

'Yes,' said Michael. 'The priest told us that Saint Cadwaladr lived during a time of plague and war. He gave everything he had to care for the poor and suffering. He is special today as the Patron Saint of the Wales Orthodox mission.'

'When we stand before that icon,' said Anna, 'we can feel that Saint Cadwaladr the last Celtic King of Britain is really here with us.'

In the sitting room Anna and Michael pointed to an icon of a holy-looking woman, with a halo of light around her head. 'Here is another ancient saint of Wales,' said Anna. 'Here is Saint Melangell, the Abbess. Saint Melangell's shrine at Pennant is still a great centre for pilgrimage.'

Michael continued the story. 'The Prince of Powys and his friends were chasing a hare with their dogs when it disappeared in a thicket of thorns. The prince hacked a path into the thicket and saw Saint Melangell praying. Sitting beside her, fearlessly, was the hare. The prince was convinced that the hare had divine protection because of Melangell's devotion to God. He gave that piece of land to Saint Melangell to build a hermitage, offering a place to pray and shelter.

'When we stand before that icon,' said Anna, 'we can feel that Saint Melangell the Abbess is really here with us.'

Then Anna and Michael took Rees and Sara to stand quietly in front of the icon in the hall. 'This is Saint Mary, the mother of God,' said Anna.

'Saint Mary is very special in our church,' said Michael. 'We call Saint Mary "the mother of God" because she gave birth to Jesus.'

'Saint Mary is very special,' added Anna, 'because Jesus is truly God as well as truly man. Saint Mary, the mother of God, gave birth to the Son of God.'

'When we stand here before that icon,' said Michael, 'we can feel that Saint Mary, the mother of God, is really here with us.'

Rees and Sara enjoyed hearing the stories of the saints shown on the icons and about the devotion of the iconographers who make the icons. They understood that icons are much more than ordinary pictures. Icons help people to pray and they draw them closer to God.

4 Helping others

It was a bright, sunny morning in late winter. A crisp layer of frost sparkled on the gardens and rooftops. It was a day full of exciting things that could happen. It was just a matter of choosing what exciting thing to do.

Rees and Sara were sipping orange juice in Anna and Michael's kitchen.

'We could go swimming or watch a film?' suggested Rees.

'Or, we could play the game that I got for my birthday,' said Anna.

Suddenly, there was a soft thud and a metallic rap of a letterbox. Seconds later, Anna and Michael's father walked in, waving a bulging letter.

'It is from your aunt in Russia!' he announced to Anna and Michael.

Then, addressing Rees and Sara, he explained, 'Anna and Michael's aunt belongs to a special community in St Petersburg, Russia. The community is an Eastern Orthodox charity organisation. They take the commandment in the Bible to love God and to love your neighbour very seriously indeed. You can see this in the work that they do. I will read the letter to you and we can see what the community has been doing.'

Dear all,

Our work in the hospital is going well. We still have the same problems, though. The hospital is not given enough money to look after its patients properly. Many of them are old and homeless. Our community does everything it can to help the hospital and to try to make things better there. I have enclosed some photographs which show some of our work in the hospital.

The first picture shows one of our sisters on duty on a hospital ward. She is helping the hospital to look after its patients. Our sisters care for the whole of the patient. They care for the patient's body, which is sick, and they also care for the patient's spirit, which people often forget about.

The sisters look after the patients' spiritual health by praying for them. They also prepare them for the sacraments of confession and communion. We have opened a small chapel in the hospital which patients can visit, if they wish.

The community has worked hard to find people who generously donate money to us. This money makes all our hospital work possible. We even use some of it to pay for basic things like medical equipment, medicines, and bed linen. The donations also support some of our other projects.

Some of the photographs show our community working with elderly homeless people in St Petersburg. These people need to be cared for in a nursing home. But it is not easy for them to get a place in a nursing home here because you have to fill in forms. Many of them find this extremely difficult. So, we help them with the forms. We can even provide some elderly homeless people with a place to stay, while they wait to hear from the nursing homes.

We have also opened two of our own nursing homes which look after some of the elderly homeless people. I hope that this tells you a little about our mission to the sick, elderly, and homeless people of St Petersburg. I will write again soon.

Aunt Natasha

Rees and Sara and Anna and Michael were very impressed with the work of Aunt Natasha's community. They thought about how easy it is to forget about the very poor, especially if they are old, sick, and homeless.

Looking outside through the window, the children could see that it was still a beautiful day, full of exciting things that could happen.

'I have an idea,' offered Sara. 'Our grandmother has not been well recently. We could visit her. She always likes company.'

Everyone agreed and thought that it was an excellent idea.

Rees and Sara enjoyed their day with Anna and Michael. They had learnt that Eastern Orthodox Christians try to help those who most need it. This is what the Bible teaches: love God and your neighbour. Anna and Michael also believe that people need more than just their bodies looking after. They need their spirits looking after too.

5 Fairtrade and Traidcraft

Well before the end of November Rees and Sara were already thinking about Christmas. Sara was dreaming about finding a skateboard all brightly wrapped under the Christmas tree. Rees was dreaming about finding a drum kit.

In their spare time Rees and Sara had already started to make Christmas decorations for their home. They had begun to make special Christmas cards to send to their friends.

In the town the big shops were already displaying their Christmas wares and tempting the shoppers to splash out on expensive gifts. Some were even playing Christmas songs.

Things were very different, however, in their local corner shop. Mr and Mrs Maslov had made a real effort to tidy the shelves, the floor, and the counter.

A lot of things had been hidden away in the storeroom at the back to make room for a special Christmas display. Here there were no Santa Claus, no sleigh, no reindeer. Here there were no expensive designer labels to tempt the shoppers.

Instead there were two beautiful displays. One was labelled 'Fairtrade' and the other 'Traidcraft'. Rees and Sara looked at the displays with a mixture of admiration and puzzlement.

'What has all that got to do with Christmas?' Rees asked his friends Anna and Michael.

Anna ignored Rees's question, led him across to the first display of chocolate and gave him a bar of elegantly wrapped dark chocolate to hold. The wrapper said 'Choco-Fair'.

'Look at that,' she said, 'that is special fairtrade chocolate.'

Rees looked at the tempting bar of chocolate resting in his outstretched hands. Then he gazed at all the different types of chocolate called 'Choco-Fair' displayed in the shop.

Above the chocolate there was a notice which Rees read out loud.
>Do you know where chocolate comes from?
>Do you know how little many of the producers earn?
>Fair-traded chocolate tries to pay them a fair wage.
>Your purchase helps them to live.

All the children were quiet and thoughtful.

Mrs Maslov went into the room behind the shop to make a drink for everyone.

Rees chose banana milkshake. The wrapping around the bananas said that they were fairtrade from the Windward Isles.

Sara chose tea with milk and a little sugar. The packet said that the tea was fairtrade from Tanzania.

Rees and Sara noticed that the Demerara sugar was fairtrade from Mauritius.

'The Eastern Orthodox Church teaches us that all people are equal in God's eyes,' said Mrs Maslov, sipping her coffee. 'We do not believe that it is right that half the world is rich and the other half is poor. This is the reason why we try to choose fairtrade products to help make things a little bit fairer across the world.'

Mrs Maslov drew Rees and Sara's attention to the second display.

'Fairtrade products are not just food products,' she said. 'Many other products are also fairtrade.'

Michael gave Sara a precious hand-painted ceramic plate to hold from the display. The label said 'Made in Thailand'.

'This is fair-traded pottery,' Michael said.

Sara looked at the fine plate resting in her hands. Then she gazed at all the different things in the display and read their labels.

The hand-made ceramic figures of Mary and Joseph came from Peru. The gold-wire Christmas tree had been hand-made in the Philippines. The pressed flower cards came from Mauritius. The silky Christmas baubles came from India.

'All these things,' said Michael, 'have been made by people living in poor countries and they have been paid a fair wage for them.'

All the children were quiet and thoughtful.

The corner shop stocked fairtrade products all the year round. At Christmas, though, there was a special attempt to encourage people to buy them.

Mrs Maslov explained, 'Jesus was born in Bethlehem to poor parents living in hard times. He was born in a stable because there was no room in the inn. When Jesus grew up he spent a lot of time teaching and helping the poor and the outcasts. The celebration of Jesus' birth at Christmas is a special time to help the poor.'

In the shop Rees and Sara had learnt that Anna and Michael's family try to help the poor and those who are treated unfairly. This is why they support fairtrade products. By doing this, they are following Jesus' example.

As Rees and Sara walked home, they agreed that they wanted to share some of their own special things with Anna and Michael. What these things are is another story.

In the World Faiths Today Series Rees and Sara learn about the major world faiths in their own country. The seven stories in the series are:

- Exploring Islam
- Exploring Judaism
- Exploring the Parish Church
- Exploring the Orthodox Church
- Exploring Hinduism
- Exploring Buddhism
- Exploring Sikhism

Welsh National Centre for Religious Education
Bangor University
Bangor
Gwynedd
Wales

© Welsh National Centre for Religious Education, 2008.

All rights reserved. These materials are subject to copyright and may not be reproduced or published without the permission of the copyright owner.

First published 2008.

Sponsored by the Welsh Assembly Government.

British Library Cataloguing-in-Publication Data
A catalogue record for this book is available from the British Library.

ISBN 978-1-85357-184-8

Printed and bound in Wales by Gwasg Dwyfor.